Autumn Manuscripts

Autumn Manuscripts
Tasos Leivaditis
Translated by
NN Trakakis

Smokestack Books
1 Lake Terrace
Grewelthorpe
Ripon
HG4 3BU
e-mail: info@smokestack-books.co.uk
www.smokestack-books.co.uk

Copyright © 2020
Stylianos-Petros Halas
for the original Greek poems

Copyright © 2020
NN Trakakis
for the Introduction and translation

ISBN 9781916139268

Smokestack Books
is represented
by Inpress Ltd

Contents

Introduction	11

I

Street Song	23
The Bird with the Truths	24
Pages of the Calendar	25
The First Verse	26
November Wind	27
Correspondence	28
Sleepless Nights	29
Yellowed Papers	30
The Scent of the Night	31
The Indistinct Figure	32
Twilight Hour	33
The Question	34
Short Autobiography	35
Disclosures	36
Ash	37
Departure	38
The Photographer	39
Young Polish Woman	40
Journeys	41
Afternoon Commentary	42
Elegy for a Young Housemaid Who Grew Up	43
The Musician with the Wide Hat	44
Travellers	45
Full Moon at the Post Office	46
The Ballad of the Trains	47
The Constellation of Leo	48
The Treasure	49
Return	50
The Secret	51
The Lovely Stationmaster	52
He Who Falls Silent	53
Unforgettable James	54

Twilight	55
The Rose	56
Questions	57
Miss Eurydice	58
Hydrangeas	59
Street Music	60
Captivity	61
Farewell	62
The Family Home	63
Of the Countryside	64
Cranes	65
The Beautiful Chrysanthemums	66
Hymn to Liberty	67
Dedication	68
Pages of Sleep	69
Small Night Time Reverie	70
The Final Hand	71
The Box with the Toys	72
Pancakes	73
Conquering the World	74
Roving Salesman	75

II

Advice to Young Writers	79
The Short Life	80
The Woman in Blue	81
The Alibi	82
The Traveller's Star	83
Time	84
After the Rain	85
Storms	86
What Shall We Do in Winter?	87
Coming of Age	88
Adventure	89
Great Eras	90
Teresa	91
Incident	92
Indescribable Dreams	93

Adolescence	94
Daybreak	95
Childhood	96
Passer-by	97
Predetermination	98
Hope	99
The Past	100
The First Day of The World	101
Tales	102
Trojan War	103
Stories	104
Autumn	105
A Bird at the Window	106
Scenes from Life	107
The Kingdom	108
Greetings to History	109
Morning Gaiety	110
The Stranger	111
The Blind Musician	112
Whistling Like a Child	113
Oddities	114
Sunset	115

III

Immortality	119
Ideologue	120
Ideologue II	121
Odyssey	122
Abridged Iliad	123
Oleanders	124
Wedding Night	125
Above All, Quiet!	126
The Dream	127
Correspondence Interrupted	128
Autumn Twilight	129
The Midnight Train	130
Futile Decisions	131
The Great Hour	132

The Ship	133
January – April – July – September	134
A Painter Who Died in Patmos	135
Disappearances	136
People...	137
Poets	138
The Garden	139
The Way	140
Simile	141
Wandering	142
Epilogue	143
Poetry is for Two	144
Summer	145
Nuptials	146
Thought at Twilight	147
Painting	148
Unknown Homeric Verses	149
Schooling	150
Lethal Game	151
Thoughts	152
New Geography	153
Simple Verses	154
Thank You	155
March	156
Tears	157
Verses	158
Oh Sorrow...	159
The Poet's Grievance	160
Acknowledgements	161
Notes	162

Introduction

'There is the waste of an all-too-rich autumn in this book: you trip over truths. You even crush some to death, there are too many of them.' That is how Nietzsche, in *Ecce Homo*, sums up the substance of a work written only months earlier, in the fateful year of 1888: *Twilight of the Idols*.[1] As the title, borrowed from Wagner's opera, suggests, this is a work of endings and crises, fall and loss, but also movement and transition. Its prodigious truths are devastating, shattering the idols of a sick and decadent civilization, and leaving one disorientated, struggling not to sink in the seas of nihilism. Herein lies the continuing appeal of Nietzsche, as the twentieth-century Nietzschean, Emil Cioran, noted (with possibly his German forebear in mind): 'I read him for the shipwrecked feeling I get from anything he writes.'[2] This, precisely, is the experience generated by another masterful book of endings and sunsets, of the disappearance of the summer sun and the turn to a light more muted and melancholy and therefore more mysterious and poetical: Tasos Leivaditis' *Autumn Manuscripts*.

Leivaditis himself died in autumn, on 30 October 1988, aged only 66. *Autumn Manuscripts*, his twenty-second book of poetry, was virtually finished by this time: the only outstanding matter was the choice of titles for some poems. But before he could submit the manuscript to the publisher, he was forced to attend to his deteriorating health. This was a problem he had been battling for some years, but typically never spoke about it to anyone. It was only during a hospital visit to his lifelong friend and mentor, Yannis Ritsos, that he disclosed his failing health to his fellow poet. Ritsos persuaded him to undergo examination by the doctors there, and Leivaditis was quickly diagnosed with an abdominal aortic aneurism and required to undergo surgery. Given the state of the recently established National Health Service in Greece, friends tried to convince him to undergo the procedure abroad (just as the leader of the nation, Andreas Papandreou, had done a few weeks earlier in choosing to go to London for heart surgery). But Leivaditis refused, and in the seven-hour operation the procedure was botched. A second operation soon followed, running a further six hours, but again there was no success. Early that Sunday morning, Greece lost one of its greatest writers.

Accorded a state funeral, Leivaditis was buried in the First Cemetery of Athens, on a cold and rainy autumn day. In attendance, along with prominent politicians and old comrades, was Ritsos, clasping the arm of Leivaditis' bereaved wife, Maria, at the head of the procession. In a short poem written only a week prior to Leivaditis' death, Ritsos wrote:

> Rain all day.
> Kids stand at the bus stops
> getting drenched.
> And you at your window –
> doing your best to alchemize
> raindrop
> into diamond.[3]

This diamond, it could be argued, was *Autumn Manuscripts*, published posthumously in Athens (by Kedros) in 1990.

The span of Leivaditis' life coincides with and indeed recapitulates the life of that superpower now long-dead: the Soviet Union. The year of Leivaditis' birth, 1922, was also marked by the birth of the Soviet Union. Inspired by the 1917 revolution, the former empire of the tsars was transformed in December 1922 into the USSR with the unification of four socialist republics. Although Leivaditis lived nearly all his life in Athens and never travelled overseas, his deepest inspiration came from Russia, particularly its writers and revolutionaries. But as the twentieth century was drawing to a close, communism also seemed to be at an end – in the Soviet Union and the Eastern Bloc, but also amongst many who had struggled and suffered tremendously on behalf of the left, Leivaditis included.

It was while studying law at university that Leivaditis turned to politics, joining in 1943 the Greek communist resistance that was fighting not only the invading German forces but also fellow right-wing Greeks in a civil war. In 1948, as the internal conflict was still raging, Leivaditis and countless other leftists (including Ritsos) were arrested and imprisoned in concentration camps on various islands. Upon his release, more than three years later, Leivaditis published his first poetry collections which, despite the recent defeat of the left in the civil war, continued the commitment to the cause. But soon enough this commitment began to wane, especially after 1956 with Khrushchev's revelations of Stalin's crimes and, later that year, the Soviet crushing of the Hungarian uprising (inspired ironically by the spirit of criticism seemingly opened by Khrushchev). These were pivotal events for many leftists in Greece and abroad: a case in point was Jean-Paul Sartre, who met Leivaditis during a visit to Athens in 1956, and that same year broke definitively with the French Communist Party and the USSR after the Soviet tanks entered Budapest, stating in *L'Express*: 'What the Hungarian people is teaching us with its blood is the complete failure of socialism as merchandise imported from the USSR.'[4]

Influenced perhaps by his French contemporary, Leivaditis did not abandon the left but took a more existentialist direction: the solitary individual, hopes for utopia dashed, now seeks clarity and connection in an unresponsive and indeed 'absurd' world. This turn in Leivaditis was consolidated during another terrible period of persecution, the military dictatorship in Greece from 1967 to 1974, when Leivaditis lost his position as literary critic for a leftist newspaper after it was shut down by the censors. Towards the end of the dictatorship, as the censors relaxed their grip, Leivaditis released *Night Visitor* in 1972, ushering what many critics regard as a new phase in his oeuvre. Stylistically the writing becomes more allusive, symbolic, introspective, lyrical, and condensed (as reflected in the prevalence of the prose-poem format), with a propensity to suddenly switch 'dimensions', from reality to dream, from memory to fantasy, from the dead to the living. Philosophically the change is manifested in many ways, but it can be largely characterized as a move from *belief* to *doubt*.

The '*metapoliteusi*' ('political transformation') begun in 1974 witnessed the restoration of (participatory, pluralistic) democracy in Greece. This signalled a promising shift away from the country's violent past (which included eight military coups over the last century), as well as increasing liberalization and secularization, and the incorporation of previously marginalized strata – especially leftist groups –into the political system and wider community. Despite these progressive institutional and cultural changes in Greek society, the work of the so-called first postwar generation –which, apart from Leivaditis, also included such distinguished writers as Takis Sinopoulos (1917–81), Aris Alexandrou (1922–78), Manolis Anagnostakis (1925–2005), and Titos Patrikios (b.1928) – became increasingly sceptical and disillusioned with all ideologies, both left and right.

As Leivaditis' generation came to see first-hand, Causes (from the Enlightenment 'metanarratives' of historical progress to political ideologies like communism and capitalism) are inevitably lost causes, doomed to failure because they cannot accommodate the vagaries and frailties of life. For Leivaditis, the loss of belief was felt as a wounding defeat, if not also as a betrayal by the very cause for which he sacrificed his youth. In work after work published after the reinstatement of democracy – and, in particular, in the three greatest works of this period: *Euthanasia Manual* (the State Poetry Prize winner of 1979), *The Blind Man with the Lamp* (1983), and *Violets for a Season* (1985) – Leivaditis gives pained expression to the 'broken dreams and dead music,' to 'that great error in which we took refuge,' while observing that 'the protest march had just finished and the police officers were erasing an entire revolution that was written on the walls...' These excerpts from *The Blind Man with the Lamp*, however, only tell half the story. For if the ready-made solutions of the past are no longer credible, it's not clear what could take their place. As Leivaditis put it in the final lines of a poem entitled 'The Key to the Mystery,' from *Euthanasia Manual*:

> ...but how many questions in the world have answers?
> and honesty always begins there, where all other paths to
>   salvation have come to an end.

This newfound sense of honesty and authenticity leads to an acknowledgement of 'mystery', but not as conceived in the dogmatic tradition of the Orthodox Church where the recognition of human ignorance and fallenness is merely a precondition for a divine disclosure of the truth. For Leivaditis, as for the French existentialists, such leaps of faith are signs of 'bad faith', the desire to flee from the contingency and meaninglessness of existence. Truth is elusive, the world is desolate, the other is inscrutable:

> One morning a bird sat on the tree opposite and
>   whistled something.
> Oh, if only I understood what it wanted to tell me,
>   perhaps I would have found the meaning of
>   the world.

These lines, from the end of 'The Bird with the Truths' in *Autumn Manuscripts*, also come from 'the end of history and the last man', to borrow from the title of Francis Fukuyama's influential 1992 book. The year following Leivaditis' death, 1989, has been described a 'caesura in history', triggered by the dissolution in rapid succession of all communist regimes in Eastern Europe, and the breakup of the Soviet Union two years later. The fall of communism brought an end to a political order (the Cold War) that had been in place since the Second World War, with wide-ranging ramifications beyond Europe, as regimes (e.g., in Afghanistan and Ethiopia) that had relied on the support of the Soviet Union collapsed, while a new imperialism (variously labelled 'neoliberalism', 'globalization', 'the Washington Consensus', or even 'liberal democracy') led by the United States and its allies began to dominate the political and economic landscape. It is amidst this combination of the demise of an old empire and the rise of an equally dangerous one that Leivaditis' *Autumn Manuscripts* appeared, opening up a space for 'the outsider', who like Camus' *étranger* resists ideals and systems, has little faith in faith, and (borrowing from a comment Camus made in one of his notebooks) knows how to speak only of what he has experienced – above all, the experience of doubt and despair.

This scepticism and anguish (not to be confused with cynicism or defeatism) pervading Leivaditis' later work finds expression in *Autumn Manuscripts* primarily in a temporal mode: the title itself gives this away, and it is reinforced in the pages that follow, with images of the season (the light and the leaves, in particular) of autumn predominating, which in turn link up with further temporal signifiers: twilight, nightfall, clocks, calendars, journeys to the past (especially to childhood). These are common tropes in literature, and autumn has long been a beloved subject and symbol for poets of a romantic bent. Think, for example, of Keats' 'To Autumn', composed as summer was fading, in 1819 (the year in which all his finest poetry was written), and as his own health was beginning to take a turn for the worse due to tuberculosis. In this period of 'the poet's own autumn,' as it has been called, Keats seeks to come to terms with the finality of mortality: after the repletion of harvest comes emptiness, after plentiful light and food come the mournful sounds and colours of the 'soft-dying day' and its 'rosy hue', while the full-reaped stubble plains and migrating swallows foreshadow the approach of winter. But within death and desertion an unparalleled beauty is discovered. As Keats explained about the mid-September walk which inspired the ode:

> How beautiful the season is now – How fine the air. A temperate sharpness about it. Really, without joking, chaste weather – Dian skies – I never lik'd stubble-fields so much as now – Aye better than the chilly green of the Spring. Somehow a stubble-plain looks warm – in the same way that some pictures look warm – This struck me so much in my Sunday's walk that I composed upon it.[5]

Helen Vendler, who thinks of Keats' 'To Autumn' as 'his finest ode', rightly reads the poem as *a defence of autumn* against other seasons, spring especially.[6] Darkness has its own light, sorrow its own song, as Keats reminds Autumn herself:

> Where are the songs of spring? Ay, Where are they?
> Think not of them, thou hast thy music too, –

These lines might function as the motto of Leivaditis' own swan song, *Autumn Manuscripts*. Although the pessimistic tone of Leivaditis' work has led critics to place him within the postwar movement in Greece known as 'the poetry of defeat' (which arose from the defeat of the communists in the civil war and the ensuing crisis in the leftist resistance), Leivaditis himself reproached the genre 'for lacking a deeper problematization and a creative employment of Marxism. For although it certainly expresses a period of history, it also cultivates the illusion that this period and this psychology will remain unchanged forever, as though the movement of History had come to a complete stop.'[7] The greatest human need or wish, Leivaditis goes on to say, is to transform the world, and art helps achieve this by bringing us to a higher level of sensibility and understanding. Leivaditis, then, never gave up on the revolutionary potential of poetry, even if the revolution was reconceived in terms of aesthetic revelation. Even if, in Leivaditis, life is presented as chaotic and illogical, history as replete with suffering and tragedy, the self as divided and conflicted with 'no exit' available, defeat is never definitive. Sonia Ilinskaya, one of Leivaditis' best readers, has emphasized how the 'specific moral sensibility and demandingness' of the genre of the poetry of defeat allowed it 'to develop into something different from itself, into a poetry of Anti-defeat.'[8] Just as Camus' consciousness of absurdity leads him to passionate revolt rather than suicide, so with Leivaditis loss and defeat pave the way to a new way of seeing and being. This is why Geoffrey Hartman's perceptive comment on Keats' ode applies equally well to Leivaditis:

> 'To Autumn' has no defeat in it. It is the most negative capable of all of Keats's great poems. Even its so-called death-stanza expresses no rush toward death, no clasping of darkness as a bride, or quasi-oriental ecstasy. Its word-consciousness, its mind's weather – all remains Hesperian.[9]

Keats is therefore addressing the figure of Autumn as much as the Hesperides, the nymphs of the evening. Hartmann detects in Keats' ode 'a *westerly drift* like the sun,' and observes that 'westering here is a spiritual movement, one that tempers visionariness into surmise and the lust for epiphany into finer-toned repetitions. We do not find ourselves in a temple but rather in Tempe "twixt sleepe and wake".[10] This association of autumn and twilight would also be made by the French symbolist poet, Stéphane Mallarmé, in his prose-poem, 'Autumn Complaint' (published in 1864 and dedicated to Baudelaire, a pioneer of modern prose-poetry):

> I have loved strangely and peculiarly all that is suggested in the word *fall* [French: *chute*]. My favourite time of year is the last languid days of summer, the cusp of autumn – and of the day, my hour of stroll while the sun hesitates before disappearing, its rays brazen on gray walls and on windows coppery. In literature likewise, my spirit's voluptuous insistence remains in the poetic death-throes of Rome's last moments...[11]

Mallarmé finds in '*chute*' loss and loneliness (the poem begins with the death of Mallarmé's sister), the mellow moods of autumn (e.g., languor and melancholy) which induce tristful dreaming but also decadence, the fall of Rome, and even the Fall. These varied resonances of 'fall' reverberate in Leivaditis' yellowed manuscript, which is similarly situated in the ambivalence of an in-between time: not quite autumn, not quite sundown, 'the sun *hesitates*'.

It is such indeterminacy and uncertainty, 'westering' and surmise, that are evoked by Leivaditis' many references to both autumn and twilight in this volume, sometimes in the same poem (as with 'Autumn Twilight'). Just as the hard, clear-cut contours of the day are overtaken by blurred outlines and quivering rays, so the loss of absolutes brings with it a loss of clarity and a surge of doubts. If, as philosophers from Plato to Heidegger have thought, to be is to be in-between – between being and nonbeing, between the gods and the beasts, between heaven and hell – then our being is inevitably inscribed by question-marks like those that fill these pages: 'What, then, did we gain? What will remain? How will we be saved?' ('Sleepless Nights'); 'What really would I do if I could start my life all over again?' ('The Question'); or simply 'Why?' ('The Photographer'). But answers to these relentless questions are not forthcoming: 'the gardens put to us unanswerable questions with roses or jasmine' ('Questions'). And so we are condemned to 'the eternal wandering' in the twilight, which also forms the backdrop to encounters with strangers, incomprehensible messages, and in 'Thought at Twilight' to the 'great secret' lying within each of us which no one, 'neither we, nor anyone else', will ever find out what it is. All that remains clear as night falls is 'everything that's unknown' ('He Who Falls Silent').

Twilight is also 'the violet hour', in TS Eliot's phrase from *The Waste Land*, a time when life and hope are swiftly perishing, and hence 'a time for confessions', as Leivaditis says ('Yellowed Papers'), taking the time to review one's past and find or create some semblance of sense. But the feeling of nostalgia and the call for apologia only produce tears and remorse, perplexity and sorrow, possibly even driving one in old age to 'resort to a mad gesture: suicide' so as to meet one's young self again ('Hymn to Liberty'). By the end, as in Samuel Beckett's *Krapp's Last Tape*, we are finished with everything, with all gods and all loves. There will be no more tapes, no more manuscripts. But the darkening dusk, for Leivaditis, is laden with possibility – the possibility of beauty born from sorrow. The best evidence for this resides in what I have elsewhere dubbed Leivaditis' 'credo', 'The Scent of the Night'.[12] This masterful creation begins with scenes of intense isolation (the narrator dials a number at random in the hope of hearing another voice), complete failure ('everything was wrong: the roads we took and the words we spoke / and the hands we held'), and oblivion (names on tombstones eroded by time) – in short, a world that eludes our longing for meaning and communion: 'We are all leaving, without anyone learning anything about anyone else.' Despite this, or (better) because of all this, Leivaditis does not end on a purely negative note, but keeps open the possibility of a beauty which, however fragile and fleeting, has the power like the conflagration of twilight (in 'A Painter Who Died In Patmos') to burn the rope with which we persistently try to hang ourselves. For this reason the late poem by Ritsos, aptly titled 'Autumn Duty', may well have been addressed to his younger and much loved companion:

And you, in the obstinacy of storms and rain,
by the lamplight, in this uncomfortable chair,
insist on leaving something for those to come – just a
    verse or two
written by the hand of rain that trembles as it points
    always at the sun.[13]

NN Trakakis

Notes

[1] See Friedrich Nietzsche, *Ecce Homo*, second section of chapter on *Twilight of the Idols*.
[2] EM Cioran, *The Trouble with Being Born*, trans. Richard Howard (Arcade Publishing, 1998).
[3] 'Ticks of the Clock no. 77' in *Late into the Night: The Last Poems of Yannis Ritsos*, trans. Martin McKinsey (Oberlin College Press, 1995).
[4] Interview in *L'Express*, 9 November 1956.
[5] Keats, letter to John Hamilton Reynolds, 21 September 1819, in *The Letters of John Keats*, 4th ed., edited by Maurice Buxton Forman (OUP, 1952).
[6] Helen Vendler, *The Odes of John Keats* (The Belknap Press of Harvard University Press, 1983).
[7] Tasos Leivaditis, 'The Poetry of Defeat: A Further Exploration', *Epitheorisi Technis*, vol. 141, September 1966, translation mine.
[8] Sonia Ilinskaya, *The Fate of a Generation: A Contribution to the Study of Postwar Political Poetry in Greece*, 6th ed. (Kedros, 1986), translation mine.
[9] Geoffrey H Hartman, 'Poem and Ideology: A Study of Keats's "To Autumn"', in Harold Bloom (ed.), *The Odes of Keats* (Chelsea House Publishers, 1987).
[10] Hartman, *ibid*, emphasis in original.
[11] I am quoting here from Keith Waldrop's translation, in his introduction to Charles Baudelaire, *Paris Spleen: Little Poems in Prose* (Wesleyan University Press, 2009).
[12] See my 'Found in Translation: On Translating Tasos Leivaditis,' *Australian Poetry Journal*, vol. 5, no. 1, 2015.
[13] Published originally in Ritsos' *The Bare Tree* (1987). The above translation is from *Yannis Ritsos: Selected Poems (1935–1989)*, trans. George Pilitsis (Hellenic College Press, 2001).

I

*I'm afraid of no one but God –
except when I serve him.
And Poetry –
even when I serve it.*

Street Song

The garden railings are wet from the rain like the poor who
    are left outside
but as night falls a flute somewhere or a star pleads for all
    humanity –
when we were children we would hide under the stairs and
    whenever we came out we'd leave behind a royal
    destiny
silence makes the world bigger, sorrow makes it more just
and later in youth we embraced the first tree and told it about
    the past
joyless days: you went away and yet you left behind a
    moving memory
and I who was mad about the future now look anxiously at
    the advancing hands of the clocks.

One night meanwhile someone walks along the street singing.
    Where have you heard that song before? You can't
    remember.
And yet the nostalgia for everything you had dreamed
    trembles within the song. You stand by the window
and listen spellbound. And suddenly at the turn of the road
    the song vanishes. Everything disappears. Silence.
Now what will you do?

The Bird with the Truths

Oblivion has covered the past, the unknown besieges the house
phantoms of things we loved and lost
and now only spiders know what comes next – but nostalgia for
    the unknown had won us over since childhood, and
        loneliness had promised us great distances.
Oh the children we were with those long neckties
    for a childhood so short!
And the evening breeze blew away the ribbons in Maria's hat
    to other constellations – we never reached her.
And I loved with passion all things I was not destined to know.
And I lived all my life in a dream
    and immortality in a few cognacs.

One morning a bird sat on the tree opposite and whistled
    something.
Oh, if only I understood what it wanted to tell me, perhaps I
    would have found the meaning of the world.

Pages of the Calendar

Who knows what will happen tomorrow, or whoever learned what happened yesterday?
my years were lost here and there, in rooms, in trains, in dreams
but sometimes the voice of a woman as night falls resembles the farewell of a part of life that has come to an end
and the days you lack, oh February, perhaps they will be returned to us in paradise –
I think about the small hotels where I scattered the sighs of my youth
until in the end no one escapes, but where would they go anyway?
and eros is our mad hope in the face of the impossibility that one person may come to know another –
Lord, you have treated poets unjustly by giving them only one world,
and when I die I want to be buried in a pile of calendar pages so that I might take time with me.

And perhaps whatever of us remains will lie by the edge of our path: a small forget-me-not.

The First Verse

But why at times do we stand in the middle of an unknown street or before an old house? What do they remind us of? Who are we looking for?
At other times under a bridge or behind a curtain you feel that you more truly exist – things that you will repay someday with your soul.
Until one morning the first birdsong in the garden could be heard. Spring.
Mother would change her hat, the young maidservant would go up to the attic to cry and grandfather would forget to read the Bible...

Now I sit in the old rocking chair where three generations sat. Where have so many people gone?
My entire life was nothing but the remembrance of a dream within another dream. And when Anna laughed it was as though she were sprinkling jasmine flowers
and for a moment the night was illumined.

I remember when, a child still, I wrote my first verse.
Since then I have known that I will never die –
                                        and that I will die every day.

November Wind

But now it's night. Let's close the door and close the curtains
because the time of review has arrived. What have we done in
 our life? Who are we? Why you and not me?
For some time now no one has knocked on our door and the
 postman hasn't shown up in centuries. Ah, so many
 letters, so many poems
swept away by the November wind! And if I lost my life
I lost it for trivial things: a word or a key, a yesterday or a
 tomorrow
but my nights always have the aroma of violets
because I remember. So many friends left without leaving an
 address, so many words without any response
and music, I think to myself, is the sadness of those who never
 had the chance to love.

Until in the end nothing remains from the past but a hazy
 memory (when did we live?)
and every time spring arrives I cry because in a short while we
 will leave and no one will remember us.

Correspondence

The birds leave in autumn, flying away to deal with mysterious
    affairs – in spring we will hear the news
in the afternoon the voices of children playing resemble a fairy
    tale which they never finished reading to us and which
    returns to seek us out
or when I hear a flute playing in the evening I think to myself
    that everything will someday end.
I sit in a coffee-house as it rains, as people grow older they
    become more foreign
and I notice some despondent people waiting at the train
    station, not for the journey but for the dream,
while drops of rain form a great epistle on the windows.
    Who sends it? What does it say? Will you reply?

Sleepless Nights

At night I usually sit down and tell myself made-up stories
or I would go to the garden that was drawn on the old side of
 the wall – spring is eternal there –
do you remember when we were desperately searching for
 God? or we would dream about feeling the mystery of a
 maidenly afternoon,
and later came the mourning, the melancholy anniversaries,
 the ashen sky
mother would every now and again allow her embroidery to
 drop to the floor so that she could bend down to see her
 dead ones for a moment
and I would find it impossible to sleep at night, having lost my
 sleep inside a fairy tale.
What, then, did we gain? What will remain? How will we be
 saved?
In the basement were hoarded a pile of things from other eras.
 When will we forget?

Boundless childhood hours when an endless summer was not
 enough for us to go from one pomegranate tree to
 another. And oh autumn, you took us further...

Yellowed Papers

I lived captive to a secret which I wanted to discover but was afraid to
in love with the distant lights and the old men who fell asleep in their chairs
and I often went down to the basement and embraced the broken pendulum clock which had ushered in so many birthdays
or I would stand in front of the mirror, 'who are you? I don't recognize you,' I'd whisper (ah, whoever did recognize us?)
isolation hung about the empty rooms like a ghost – and see how autumn too has arrived, a time for confessions, we used to say.
Close the door and leaf through these yellowed manuscripts – therein lies all our pain
which no one finally understood – not even we.
    Oh evenings of youth
when God threw all his stars over our sleeplessness
and you, ancient and sorrowful moon, at times we think
    we hear your voice
like the voice of those we will never hear again.

The Scent Of The Night

Sometimes the isolation becomes unbearable, you then dial some phone number
just to hear a voice, you ask for someone by name, 'wrong number' comes the reply
everything was wrong: the roads we took and the words we spoke
and the hands we held… As a child I would hide behind the commode, the infinite lay there, but it couldn't contain anything other than me –
that's why I tell you let's not ask for anything more, and later, as a grown man, I would sit at the window and gaze at the city lights
in this way I came to know the inescapability of separation – what will remain, then?
what will remain from so many hopes, so many sighs?
a name and two dates engraved in stone which will be eroded by time slowly slowly.
We are all leaving, without anyone learning anything about anyone else. Why? What caused this?
Or is it possible that everything happens for some mysterious reason: an unsolved enigma perhaps, or some punishment?

But how beautiful the earth smells at night! Oh flowering futility of the world…

The Indistinct Figure

Now the years have gone and having loved all the joys of the
    world
the time has come for me to renounce them – the days pass
    quickly
and at night that indistinct figure shows up by the stairs
'what do you want?' I ask, frightened, 'my share' comes the
    reply, oh Lord and God, where am I to find a whole
    treasure to give him
for who hasn't squandered treasure in their youth?
I was so grief-stricken that my steps led me to the old family
    home or I would fall in love with a watch that had
    stopped
do you remember the romances with our cousins? so many
    summers and we never managed to explore the garden
so many autumns and we never came to know our souls
and oh the shattering of our dream: you closed all the roads so
    that you may open up a path to the unknown.

One day it will be raining and I will die from nostalgia.

Twilight Hour

We are prisoners of the inexplicable and of the eternally lost
and remorse is our only way to return to childhood purity –
oh my old departed friend, I know I'll meet you in a dream or
>suddenly in the street when everything will have been
>lost,
women we loved while outside the rain was becoming
>heavier
and later we crossed the bridge holding hands, your hair wet
>and shimmering in the sunset –
who would have thought it true that there was a time when we
>gave our lives
with that incessant fever like sick children who when they
>recover no longer fit in their small clothes
and are taunted at school – and fill their exercise books with
>poems
so that their lives are not lost. And later adulthood arrives like
>a shipwreck.

Oh twilight, fair hour, you give meaning
even to the humblest of things before night falls.

The Question

At times I think to myself: what really would I do if I could
 start my life all over again? I would have arrived here
 again
at the edge of the world. Oh Lord of the distant rail stations
 which we occasionally pass through in dreams –
no one returned from the journey: time changes you and
 someone else returns instead of you,
and those who loved fame will die unknown in the cold room
 of a hotel,
they will go up the wooden stairs, they will lock the door and
 cry
for their betrayed life. (Who betrayed them?) In the meantime
 a roving musician on the street will bribe the dusk with
 a sad song so that it may linger.
Oh my sorrowful ones, you who leafed through your days
 like the illegible pages of a book whose end you will
 never reach –
I remember the nights when we would fall silent, I would be
 seized with fright, 'and now who will ask the great
 question?' I'd think to myself.
 What question?

Maybe you must completely lose yourself in order to find out
 someday who you are...

Short Autobiography

I remember a house with a garden in some suburb, my family
    with its beautiful principles which unravelled over time
unmentionable love affairs with aunties, the elder brothers
    who would press upon the housemaids
the endless mornings with the birds singing the *Resenda*
the voluptuousness of midday, the tedium of the afternoon –
and other times my pain would become unbearable whenever
    I'd think that at some stage they will forget about me (all
    my relations had gradually disappeared)
one day I brought a woman home, I undressed her and got her
    to softly say my name
in that way I came to know all the sins – ah, I'm mad about
    posthumous fame, I'd like them to talk about me for two
    or three millennia
and not even that would be enough for me – and at night I'd
    question the moon that was sitting atop the pear trees
    (an entire life spent questioning) until dawn arrived and
    the daylight turned down the lamps.

'Now the house belongs to the dead,' I suddenly thought one
    morning. I locked up
and left amidst the dry leaves.

Disclosures

One night as I was looking at myself in the mirror I was filled with fear, 'what if I see the other inside?' I thought to myself, because in fact there was a confused narrative concerning my person, they would say many things, what to believe first? And they often claimed that I babble whereas I was simply conversing with the one who hides in the shadows.

In the end the years went by, I got lost on tough streets, I slept in dirty rooms and in the morning I hung the sheets from the window in unconditional surrender. And I remember as a child I would disclose to mother in the evenings that at school I sat at the same desk with an angel.

And one day I would like them to write on my tombstone: he lived at the border of an indeterminate age and died for distant things which he once saw in an uncertain dream.

Ash

Vile insignificant details which gradually define your life,
what life? Ambitions, loves, guilt, ancient debts have wasted
    your life away, what remained?
the ash of the departed sits atop the furniture and blurs the
    windows and mirrors
and on them I sometimes write the names of those who have
    gone
and other times I stand by the window and look at the passers-
    by heading towards oblivion
women cry as they recall whispered words from old love
    affairs
we are all desperately searching for a path, to go where?
where did we live, then? neither here nor there – cheap hotels
    in remote neighbourhoods with blinding lights and
    dirty washbasins where future murderers or suicides,
    unsuspected still, leant over and wept –

One summer night, while still a child, I went out the house
    and lay down in the garden
and as I looked up at the sky, my God! what infinitude! how
    many stars! I was panic-stricken.
Since then I have known that I won't make it in time.

Departure

The clocks strike the lost hours, but no one believes them,
ah the endless danger signals I sent and still no one has replied –
but someday I will try to remember, to remember how I got
    here,
everything happened so quickly, friends went their separate
    ways, some were lost in the war, others at the turn in the
    road
lovers got married and now grow old next to strangers
at times in the afternoon a wind arises, the shutters are
    battered like pangs of remorse – for what beautiful
    blunder, I wonder?
and childhood: a heavenly gloss on the enigma that we exist.

And when I leave someday I won't take anything with me
    other than a little violet from the twilight and a star
    from some fairy tale.

The Photographer

On my table I usually have a bulky leather-bound Bible open. In there I suspect there is some clue about the great secret that God, in his magnanimity, concealed from us so as not to add even more sorrow to our lives. But someday the stories of the earth will come to an end and I too will have to give a speech of my own. And so when the photographer arrived, I asked him 'why?' When I later observed him from the window I saw that he went and sat sadly by the shore and began to throw small rocks into the boundless sea.

Young Polish Woman

Houses full of ghosts over the silent city
pale women behind the windowpanes (what are they waiting
 for?), embalmed old men in the coffee-houses
the floor creaks with grievances, sighs arise from dying stairs
centuries-old dust on the furniture and bells that remind us of
 ancient debts
in the background the ashes from betrayed Warsaw are still
 giving off smoke –
oh why did I allow myself to grow up? how was I fooled?
a world that cannot be set to rights – and yet, remember lads?
 our days were a marvellous enigma which we
 occasionally solved in our sleep
and the piano teacher in the afternoon would play some
 Chopin after class for beautiful aunt Elvira and the
 clock would strike seven.
Later the teacher married our housemaid, aunt Elvira cried for
 days and the clock always struck seven.

Journeys

Many wonder how I lived – they don't realize that I was always
    away,
journeys to the unbelievable when we were children, journeys
    to the infinite when we were in love
journeys from one room to the other, from one star to the
    other, oh journey to the unrealizable!
and Martha in old age continued her embroidery for years
she had journeyed far into nothingness and had come back
    unblemished and unhappy –
my poor ones, as the twilight sprinkles the world with gold,
journeys are made to deserted wharves, to broken mirrors, to
    years that have disappeared
because I, you scoundrels, didn't come here to play
    but to suffer and to lose myself –
a downpour of old wings for nothing other than the mystery
    of it all.
And only poetry is not the journey
    but the bitter return.

Afternoon Commentary

Night was falling and the passers-by looked like ghosts on the windows
a child hid behind the couch, their silence is already an abyss, their solitary sensuality the most perfect form of eros,
two former lovers meet on the stairs, what do they have to say? brief explanations that deepen the inexplicable,
the time when you knock on a door just to hear a voice – nobody, they must have moved, everyone is moving house, what are they trying to escape from?
you meet someone and ask for an address, but they don't understand you, for some time now you have been speaking a language unknown to others,
keys you threw down the drain, one night you discover them on the table
mirrors in which we saw youth departing.

And then from the depths the sound of the station clock tolling eight times
that hour that will never return.

Elegy for a Young Housemaid Who Grew Up

   I usually wander through the deserted house, becoming so exhausted that the lamp I carry thinks it's moving on its own,
   and yet I was once a beautiful falling star that swept across the garden and I loved the daffodils and my name was written with lilac-coloured ink – (I don't remember why but it was so beautiful to weep in the evenings) or when they would lock me in the attic as punishment I would take with me the entire infinitude
   and the young housemaid would secretly come and throw me biscuits from the skylight – a few days ago I learned that she died in an asylum and I'm considering going to the cemetery where she reposes, old and forgotten, and to place on her tombstone some of my dubious laurels –
   oh the mystery of crying silently, the mystery of not having any more tears
   and the beautiful answer the starry sky gives to everything with its silence.

The Musician with the Wide Hat

Sometimes as you wait to hear the pendulum clock strike four or seven
those other sounds can be heard, also of four or seven, but so different. What has happened?
A nostalgia for things I never knew, a scent from old books
the colours of dusk, a voice on the street – so many years have passed and they still control your destiny
women suddenly seen at a corner or under a street lamp at night (you've grown old and haven't been able to forget them)
doors you opened forcefully, frightening the Stranger who comes to stay at every house in the evening.

And the train that came from a faraway city stopped at the deserted station
no one got off except for a musician with a wide windbeaten hat
he opened the violin case and began to play a strange kind of music
as though he wanted to convince us that everything is possible and that the world never ends.

Travellers

It would rain in the afternoon, the rain would entangle the
    ashen sky with the yellow leaves
the never with the nowhere, I would wonder about the rooms
    like a traveller who has lost his way
'hey, who are you?' I sometimes asked, 'the one you must not
    remember,' I heard someone whisper and was seized
    with fear
I searched everywhere – but what could I find in a world
    where everything is lost in advance?
Besides I had so many things to think about, but what's the
    point now that my young years are gone?
Our words routinely deceive the ineffable and yet we continue
    to speak. What do we say?
Thus I preferred to keep a calendar for the times I never got to
    know – it was a lovely reminiscence
or at night the steps of a pedestrian on the street would always
    remind me of the eternal departure.

Oh you who are shipwrecked in seas you never travelled upon!

Full Moon at the Post Office

       One evening I was standing outside a post office in a foreign city. What was I doing there? And to whom was I going to send that long letter I was holding? The full moon then appeared from the hill opposite, reminding me that I am no longer young. Afterwards I went to an arcade where the poor were selling shabby lace artefacts, at the back of a coffee-house a gas lamp was quietly whispering something – perhaps lines from Milosz.

       Wanderings in the intimacy of autumn and the ruptured fragrance of the night – I was quite forlorn for such a big sky, quite ill so as to want to forget, oh trains that passed me by, women who did not look after me, the aged Teresa no longer had any lovers and would sleep amongst the amaranth, while mother would smile sadly with only two teeth

       at the bottom of the world.

The Ballad of the Trains

When we fell into poverty uncle Elias, my father's brother, would go every morning and stand outside the shops of old workmates asking for a few drachmas or some cigarettes. His cheap trousers would tremble in the icy wind.

Afterwards he would go to a tailor's shop, he would blow upon the burning coals in the iron so as to appear likeable and then would quietly sit in the corner, but his aged lips would quiver as though he were continuing with an old story.

Later he completely lost it, he found a school bag and would carry it all day long, wandering the streets while the guardian angel of children followed him.

When he returned home he would lie down in the small upstairs bedroom, he would not switch on the light as though he wanted to come to know the darkness or how much loneliness a person can bear. And all night he would listen to the trains which passed by whistling in the distance. Where are they going? And will they ever make it?

The Constellation of Leo

It was very early in the morning when I went into the large drawing room. 'Teresa!' I shouted. No reply. I poured some more cognac and I looked in my glass, hoping to find that legendary key. That's how my alcoholism started. And as if all those adventures weren't enough for me, I had to find as quickly as possible the path that leads to the constellation of Leo. I was to deliver something important there. That's why when they mock me that all day I sit around doing nothing, there's no point explaining it to them, who would understand? I prefer to reminisce about our country house and the young housemaids who laughed nervously while grandpa caressed them behind the trees. And every time they spoke to me about God I didn't believe them, but later when I remained alone with the silence, I understood both God and his work. 'Teresa!' I again shouted. No reply.

(Just leave me in the dream, because there no one dies.)

The Treasure

Despite all my misfortunes, rumours about which would have sufficed to make me famous, I never abandoned my hopes. More still: each morning I got dressed and left the house in a triumphant spirit. I walked around the square and returned home from the back door, making sure no one was following me. To be even more positive that no passer-by would cast an envious glance through the shutters, I placed a screen in front of the window. And then I began my search. I would search for the old lost treasure, in pursuit of which billions of people have devoted their lives. And as expected my own investigations also proved to be futile. Only in my last years did I realize that my father had found the treasure. Indeed. For when he became bankrupt and everything was soon to be taken from us, he smiled, smiling as though he found something he was looking for over many years, as though he suddenly discovered that nothing belongs to us and there's no point tormenting ourselves with extraneous things...

Return

One evening as the wind blew through the open window the curtain flapped a little and then rested on the edge of the chair like a friend coming back from the place of no return. To be sure he will not stay long. It's just that I am worried. Over the last years the layout of the city has been quickly changing and soon how will our dead friends be able to find us? That's why at every street corner we must place some sign: a group of children singing, a coffee-house with lowered lights, or a watch buried in the garden. Even though they now know the time. Quiet!

The Secret

I was correcting the proofs of my two-volume treatise concerning the disastrous consequences of autumnal daydreaming (it was being issued in a third edition) when there was a knock on the door. It was the postman. At any rate I'd like to be honest as far as is humanly possible: over there no one loved me – besides who ever asked them to? As for the content of my correspondence I won't say a word, even though the temptation to do so is great. But herein lies the marvellous thing, that there is nothing marvellous. And often even during the most pleasant parties I would be tormented by the worry: in which room are the icons placed? On another occasion I was walking along a deserted street when someone approached me. 'My God, now I will find out what it is!' I thought and shuddered, referring to the secret. But that scoundrel walked by without saying anything to me. I was bathed in cold sweat. The same thing when I was a child – at one point I was living with my aunt, the train that passed nearby would rattle the house in the evening and take me with it. No one ever found out about it. And in the morning in the pale dawn I would return from my nightly adventures as innocent and unprepared as before.

The Lovely Stationmaster

I had spent the night with horrid premonitions and now I was looking through the window at the deserted street. Suddenly the stationmaster appeared. He was liked by everyone because of the lovely red stripe on his hat. I opened the window. 'Hello stationmaster!' I shouted, 'I wanted to explain to you, but I'm in a hurry now, another time.' And I closed the window. My mind then turned to a house I had lived in, almost as an intruder. Whenever I passed the bust in the hallway I shuddered, as the bust would make a small head movement, as though it too were testifying to me of the inexplicability of the world. Eventually the occupants of the house caught on and kicked me out. But perhaps this was for the best because that house was located in the country and in the country there usually are many trees – and I've no intention at all of hanging myself. I then met Elvira. We rented a small furnished room and spent most of the time talking. We particularly liked to tell each other aphorisms or enigmas. One day I said to her: 'When all things are yours, there's not a thing you could lack – therefore God exists!' And I looked at her triumphantly. However, despite all the enigmas, she had undergone many abortions. That evening she was ill and trembling from fever. I got her to lie down and placed even my coat over her blanket. 'Tell me a story,' she said. I then began to tell her about my life. I talked and talked. And suddenly I thought to myself: 'what life?' Elvira had fallen asleep. I remember it was raining. The years had passed by. I sat on the stairs and began to cry...

He Who Falls Silent

Twilight always has the sadness of an endless separation
and I lived in rented rooms, with their dark stairs which lead
    one knows not where
with middle-aged landladies who refuse, cry a little and then
    give in and the next morning they air the house to get
    rid of the great sighs
in the antique beds with knobs at the four corners many
    passers-by of this world lay down and dreamed
and then fell asleep, mellowed and uninformed, like the dead
    in the old cemeteries –
but you fall silent, why don't you talk? tell me why we came
    here? where did we come from? And those hieroglyphs
    made by the rain on the earth
what are they trying to say? Oh if only you could understand
    them, everything would change.

When in the end, after many years, I returned, I didn't find
    anything other than the same deserted streets, the same
    tobacconist shop at the corner
and everything that's unknown as night was falling.

Unforgettable James

And if over the years you have seen me at bus stops, at the corners of side streets or at railway stations, it is because I was waiting for unforgettable James, a friend I have never met despite having frequently heard his voice in a park or seen his shadow in a deserted street. Besides, the most beautiful things will remain forever unknown or without realizing it they have passed right by us and disappeared amongst the things past. Even if he is not called James, but Raphael or Matthias, Ignatius or Symeon (how many names has sorrow, how many roads has the unknown!) he will come one day, and we will talk about the lovely sensualities of summer or the travails of autumn and as night falls we will erect amidst this incomprehensible world a monument to true friendship – a friendship between two men who never met, but lived for much time close to one another.

(And poetry is the word that has been silenced so as to lead us to heavenly misunderstandings.)

Twilight

Minor details that make memories more painful
and our years, like stuffed birds, now look at us with foreign
    eyes –
and I, who was I? a prince of nothingness
someone mad about revolutions and other wasted things
and whenever the bells tolled I felt that humankind was in
    danger and rushed to rescue it.
And when a child gazes at the twilight with rapture, they are
    storing up sorrows for the future.

The Rose

The reflection of the moon on the windows – like the small
    fragments from a dream that we pursue for years.
Love for things far away, friendships with streets or stars.
And the childhood that, in its best moments, remained forever
    unknown.

One night, then, I set aside my life and found the beautiful
    rose they had promised me.

Questions

The lit up roads of the big cities terrify the pedestrians but prepare the poets, and dogs stand shivering at street corners as though they suddenly saw something in the distance – my beautiful secret, however, is that I never met Judith, and oh sleep, leaf through your book with the enchanting pictures, because we never lived and childhood was an unsolvable enigma which frightened the grown-ups, and if we loved, we loved things that flickered in the background and quickly disappeared, like the love affairs of the ill which will be short-lived but God's blessing makes them appear eternal and the gardens put to us unanswerable questions with roses or jasmine and oh thousand broken mirrors of the moon and the mad mad sea that tries to piece them together.

The world exists only when you share it...

Miss Eurydice

It was during that time that I began to exercise. For I thought to myself: I must get stronger, otherwise how will I lift that trunk full of valuables that I might chance upon on the street. Besides life passed by and that is something I'll never forgive anyone. And put aside my previous depositions: I'll tell the truth only when I want to or when they allow me to cry. One evening, then, I happened to meet Miss Eurydice. When she was young she would give piano lessons. She was a descendant of an age-old and wealthy family that went bankrupt. Later, over the years, she began to drink to the point where she would wet herself. 'Miss Eurydice, don't you remember me?' I asked her. She didn't reply. She wore a blue silk dress with a white youthful collar around her aged neck. 'Miss Eurydice, I'm the one who thought all those vile things about you,' I added. Then she smiled at me. And she gently took me by the hand and very slowly

    pulled me out of Hades.

Hydrangeas

The front doorbell was ringing insistently, I took my time to answer, relishing as always the suspense. When I opened a young man was standing outside. 'You're Arthur Rimbaud from Charleville,' I said, 'what do you want?' 'We are both in danger,' he replied. But I paid no attention. I continued getting up late in the morning, I would make tea and straighten my hat a little, for in order to lead my persecutors astray I would even wear it in my sleep. But the problem was the rest of the day. How would the hours pass? The gardener's young daughter had died in a hospital for the destitute, the prisoners would stroll around the grey courtyard without looking at the sky, and the coffee-house *The Beautiful Age*, where we would meet up in our youth, had closed down. So I would sit down and enjoy the quiet or I would browse the timetables of the trains or the ships (flying by air was still for the very bold and oblivion always for those who are lost). 'Arthur,' I said to him, 'how did you find me? No one knows who I am.' He smiled. 'I always loved hydrangeas,' he said. And we went down the stairs and took to the great roads
which lead nowhere...

Street Music

And because I still had a bit of time at my disposal I went to send off my eldest brother whose untimely death, in a curious coincidence, did not benefit him at all, like Napoleon for instance, who died in glory at Saint Helena while my brother died unknown in an aged people's home, which had so many rotted floorboards that I would forget that at one point I too was a human being. Or once when I was eating with my friend Jeremiah in the cookhouse, I asked him 'who am I, Jeremiah?' I was consumed with anxiety, 'if you buy me a drink I'll tell you,' I bought him one, 'you're a poofter,' he said, I didn't utter a word, I bowed my head and prayed, and I remember when I was a child I would cry with mother as we read *The Two Orphans* and when we returned from the cemetery where we had left her all by herself it was still raining, 'and yet, mother,' I said to her, 'we've been through a lot together.'

And so as we walk one night along the street, some music in the distance reminds us of another, unbelievable life –

When did we live it?

Captivity

Even though all my life I was in a hurry, the night would always find me unprepared or I would gather the autumn leaves, they have a mysterious fate that surpasses us and generally humane sentiments don't lift you up high, at most you will reach as far as the guillotine or even the window of a woman with red hair, and I say 'red' because I love the future, just as pharmacies at night resemble imaginary exits and poets dream about Roman festivals or refuse to die, otherwise I am usually on fire, that way I pass the winter better or whenever I was kicked out of a house I always left an axe behind the door.

But my best moments come in the evenings, when I open the window and let free the beautiful songbirds I train in endless hours of captivity.

Farewell

Migratory birds sit for a moment in the bare trees, the tower soars above the mist, there daydreamers hold a book to their chest that has yet to be written and look for an idyllic place to be buried. Oh the noise of departure and the traveller in the enclosed carriage who continues his fateful dream. A spiral staircase on the tower leads to the top floor. The beautiful woman lives there. In the evenings she comes out and sits on the balcony. Other times she goes down and takes a stroll up to the Inn of the Good Old Days. One day she will leave for a distant constellation – destiny takes care of everything. The postman comes every morning and is treated to a glass of red wine. Afterwards half of the visitors to the tower leave to go hunting. The others will die differently. The clock strikes twelve. Let's bid farewell to one another!

The Family Home

I was walking for hours. Perhaps I had overstepped all the boundaries when a house appeared in front of me. 'My God, the house I grew up in!' I whispered. I ran up the stairs, my very own mother opened the door, I was shocked, but I was embarrassed to tell her that she was dead. In her hands she held a small coffee grinder which she was given as a newly-wed. And she turned the handle of the grinder with such gravity that I nearly burst into tears. A calendar hung on the wall, and when the wind blew through the open door the calendar began to dissolve into pieces, its faded pages becoming scattered, 'why, mother?' I asked her, 'and yet you loved me.' I then noticed my brother, who had also died but for some strange reason still slept at home, our needs of course were so many that father, even though he too was dead, tried to wake him up so that he can go to work, 'but father, I work somewhere else,' my brother replied, finally before I went down the stairs I managed to catch sight of an elderly housemaid of ours from the olden days, she was dead also and was hurriedly closing the curtains in the windows of this mysterious house, whose location was unknown to me, nor would I ever discover it...

Of the Countryside

The best times we had now torment us with memories
        and we try to forget them
the rooms have become full of useless furniture, lace artefacts
        from other eras, letters that were not sent
at night the moon takes me by the hand and we return to the
        old boarding school,
from some window can be heard the harsh words between a
        couple which was once passionately in love.
Everything comes to an end and only autumn remains
        eternally young like the most melancholy poems.
I am alone. The countryside is sweet-smelling. The oncoming
        train can be heard and I lean my head on the tracks.

One day we will meet again.

Cranes

And later, when full of hope we settled into the new house and rearranged the furniture,
we noticed that there's no way to hide our old great mistake and that things have a loneliness of their own
and a justice of their own. We then opened the window and saw cranes passing by.
But what was our mistake? We never found out. And only occasionally in a nightmare do we come across some kind of answer
but we don't want to accept it. What's the point, then, of so many dreams given that everything will end someday
and no one knows when the crucial hour will come –
things you discover when it's too late (it was always too late)
and the scent of a withered rose is even more dreadful than a ghost.
Someday we will choke on these many unspeakable words.

The Beautiful Chrysanthemums

That night I was hiding behind the wardrobe,
but why should I make any disclosures? times were tough:
    revolutions, disappointments
and sometimes things happen which you recall having
    experienced before – in which dream, I wonder, or in
    which other life?
small rooms where I walked up and down across the whole of
    infinity
empty secluded roads where I experienced my most beautiful
    adventures
and when one day the time comes to defend myself, I will have
    as witnesses all the passers-by before whom I stood
    helpless,
having nothing to say. So, what became of the beautiful
    chrysanthemums?
Where did the old days go?

People who spent their lives searching by sight for the horizon.
The whistling of trains which takes you further than the trains.

Hymn to Liberty

Life is a dangerous game, especially when you play it with
    others
and the woman of the street is so ugly that out of the greatest
    idiot she could fashion a Picasso
I was so helpless that old tales would protect me
in old age I will resort to a mad gesture: suicide –
    perhaps I will meet my young self again
and that alibi I have been preparing for years will seem to me
    to have no meaning at that difficult moment
because the future has never acquitted anyone and the twilight
    bears the sorrow of centuries,
how many events we did not understand! how many thoughts
    we eventually did not utter!
and every night after I undress I go down to the town square
    and lay my clothes on the gallows,
oh infinitude, we will never come to know you, but it is you
    who confers that hidden magic
upon our lost uprisings.

Dedication

To those who in stormy nights of uprisings search for a
    childhood moon
to those who have run out of time, to those who have been
    forgotten
to the sweetness of sleep when everyone had abandoned us
to the mirrors we looked into, to the seas we will never cross
to the paths we walked upon as lovers and perhaps we have yet
    to return since then
to Fate, to beautiful youth, to pedestrians
(and where was I going? did I ask for too much? but now it's
    late – time for me to leave)
to migratory birds, to locomotives which grew tired and
    turned to the side to sleep
to corn plants when bathed by the moon, to girls who take off
    their dresses to enter the heavens,
to the exchange of letters between an angel and a child, to
    those who are late, to those who will not return
to the woman who tells the future by cards, to the old man
    who cries
to the Odyssey experienced by the poet writing the shortest
    poem
to the fleeting moment experienced by someone as life
    entire...

Pages of Sleep

Where dreams end, our lives begin
ah! how unwarily we lived – in the evening grandfather would remove the dust of the day from his frock coat
and I would doze off on the stairs of a fairy tale
or amongst the rosemaries a small lizard frightened us like a premature love –
and who's that coming from behind us? and who's that other one, the one we are following?
pages of sleep which no one knows how to read and are memorized by the birds
old waltzes on the gramophone and the starlight that swirled as we danced in the park with the beautiful cousin
and afterwards from the half-opened door we saw her putting on her nightie like a rose bush shedding all its flowers all at once –
silent enigma of the world stirred up with the evening smoke
gentle rustle of the trees as if a poet were leafing through his book.

Small Night Time Reverie

I'm generally unable to sleep at night
and I attend to the flowers drawn on the couch cover
it occurs to me that they too will one day blossom
the dead will return
the statues will remember to speak again
lovers will make peace
those who were late will recoup lost time
poets will measure the depth of the abyss.

The Final Hand

Truly, how many years ago did we sit at this table and begin
    playing the final hand?
Out there the big city, railway stations full of smoke, migrants
    crying
fire engines are the howl of hatred that ignites the great fires
roads in turmoil like the thoughts of a lunatic, windows open
    like traps
and an aged whore stands at Hagia Thekla Street with her skirt
    lifted high, revealing the sorrow of creation
the dim lights narrate stories of terror which drunkards try to
    conceal with solemn songs –
we are prisoners of a truth which was lost somewhere in our
    childhood years
and we experienced infinitude in small dark rooms and
    nothingness in the great pages of History –
what do you say? want to play one more hand? The world is an
    entirely personal matter.

The Box with the Toys

      Several days had passed since the crime when Raskolnikov warily went up the stairs and rang the bell, I opened the door, 'what do you want?' I asked, 'the box with the toys, I didn't take it with me,' he replied – finally after many years my turn came to ring the bell, Mrs Olga, no longer young, opened the door with a beautiful contralto voice, in the evenings she would sing in such a way that it was like she were throwing a white sheet upon old furniture, she showed me to the large drawing room with the yellow wallpaper covered all over with images of birds ready to sing if God so wished, and then someone began to tell a story and we listened with that innocent, all-powerful ingratitude of children
      when they recreate the world...

Pancakes

My good friend Raphael stood perplexed by the window amongst the shimmer of the sea and the lost things of old, 'Raphael, don't worry,' I said to him, 'and leave the beyond alone' – I had just come out of a long drawn-out illness and I had strange ideas: to propitiate a star, to love humanity or to succeed a poet of short tombstone inscriptions. Night fell – a time when vagrants lick their lips with the full moon which reminds them of Mrs Thekla's pancakes in the shelter and the sea penetrates deeply into the mysteries of God, because after a difficult day there always comes a night when one does not know what to do.

Conquering the World

      We set out to conquer the world – myself, a soldier from the Great War and Comte de Lautréamont. The train was travelling at breakneck speed. It was a daring plan – someday I will explain it to you. Night. The floodlit cities passed by from the windows like alight rags hounded by the wind. The count wore a large cloak so as to cover his century and a necktie agitated like an uprising. The soldier was wounded and delirious, and it was perhaps his incoherent words that explained the dream of an era. Afterwards it began to snow, we were cold just as in prehistory. 'Rachel!' the soldier whispered. What was he trying to say? The count leaned over him. 'Compassion is the only excuse for the crime that we exist,' he said.

      That's why I tell you: when you hear a train whistling at night, get up and stay up.
                              We might not see each other again.

Roving Salesman

Since then I lived without having any curiosity – curiosity
    wears you out and in the end what have you found?
but I continued to dust the empty room, 'we must preserve
    something from the beautiful youth of the past,' I would
    say –
what room and what youth, you scoundrels? you simply want
    to scare me
and the devil usually wins the bet (you too will meet him one
    night on the stairs)
as for me I always remained a roving salesman of bygone
    things, but who today would buy
umbrellas from ancient downpours or lovely days that will
    never return? – as for the rest it is a devastating matter
because when they throw you out and you're walking down
    the stairs humiliated, the angels in the heavens
are preparing your future wings – so, no need to bother, I will
    come by some other time, thank you, your servant.

II

*Oh poetry –
you are the beginning
of our great dream
and the end
of our small journey.*

Advice to Young Writers

From all sorts of personal reflections and adventures I have arrived at one conclusion and in light of this I would like to offer a piece of advice to all young people who dream of attaining the fame of a true writer. When with God's help you finish your first book, go down to the cellar and hang yourself...

The Short Life

We met outside the dark, secluded second-hand shop. It was a damp winter dusk. A clock somewhere struck five. I had not seen him before. He wore a somewhat extravagant hat and we looked each other in the eyes. What were we looking for? Perhaps everything – oh if only we had spoken! His overcoat was large enough for further sorrows. A sad song was heard coming from somewhere. The clock struck six.

Life was over!

The Woman in Blue

A woman stood at the entrance of the coffee-house. She was not waiting for anyone. No one was waiting for her. Why was she standing there? Who was she? Perhaps some old, forgotten singer. Or a woman from another era who had lost her way. No one found out. At any rate, a woman of a certain age.
And as evening approached, nothing was left in the world other than sorrow, night, desolation and that need to get by in our dark lives.

The Alibi

And only one thing I didn't understand and I hope you won't
    understand it either
because right after the dreadful moment had passed someone
    opened the door and they all left one by one. Only I
    remained.
'That too is an alibi,' I stammered. 'But who does it exonerate?'

That's the story of my life. Now I sit quietly in my room
like someone who has become estranged from everything and
    does not wait for anything and is all alone, their only
    power
to have no power at all.

The Traveller's Star

Out of a lost dream we should have created a road upon which
    to meet
and when our tears ran out we sent the birds to our dead
    friends
it was snowing, the wind was blowing and we built our house
    with a little forgetfulness
and out of all the destinies we preferred that of the traveller
    who isn't aware of his guiding star
until we were expiated like those who have been dead now for
    years.

Oh hopes of our youth: you remained in the middle of the
    road. We continued
and see how we made it here today, to this unknown land,
    without luggage but with such a beautiful moon.

Time

Then he spoke about some key.
'How incomprehensible it is to live,' he said.
In an adjoining room a beautiful woman was engrossed in the
    mirror.
Finally he talked about a seashore, an enigma and a sick
    sleeping child.
'And then what happened?' I asked.

I didn't notice that thirty years had already gone by.

After The Rain

I don't know when, I don't know whether many years ago or after my death, the letter will arrive that will intensify the confusion even more, and truly who is it that thrusts us from one year to another?
The rain stopped. The trees drip with loneliness...

Storms

Dreams of my youth that have not come true and accompany
    me still
and our friends have not died, they now simply dwell in
    autumn
the sorrow of a little Mary who departed early
the sorrow of a Metropolis that would have liked to be a
    swallow's nest
moneychangers debase the gold of the day
drunkards stagger as they lift so many tomes of misfortune
and oh fluttering eyelashes of children: suddenly in sleep it is
    as though you have been touched by the storms
that come hurriedly from the future.

What Shall We Do in Winter?

Some people were standing near the railings, their faces were not visible while their gestures were indistinct as though they were intimating something else as well, oh friendships with dark things and Mary's old worn-out coat with its large loose threads like hydrangeas, the house half-lit.

The truest stories are the ones that no one remembers.

Coming of Age

Insignificant things which we only recently noticed and
 quickly forgot,
the scent of a soaked garden, the gaze of a passer-by, the
 broken voice of a woman from some window –
we forgot them, but someday we will remember them and will
 feel as though we abandoned there in the middle of the
 road
our most beautiful destiny or a beloved dead person.
But now what can I do? I should at least own up to how old I
 am.

Adventure

Every day something ends, in this way we very slowly become accustomed to the great end
we see a hat on the lawn, a piano next to the sea, a woman in the rain –
remember the sanitorium in the remote suburb and our correspondence from adjacent rooms?
afterwards the departure and a simple farewell without further significance.
The night then arrived and the stars were the last sign that we had loved each other...

Great Eras

Whenever night falls the air smells like honeysuckle, as
 though we have been forgotten for years
trams, with the clatter of iron hitting the ground, turn the
 corner and disappear – a hallucination, of course: trams
 have been discontinued for years now.
And those who made their way in the dusk with a stoop were
 beautiful because they had been defeated.

Teresa

That night I returned anxious, 'Teresa!' I shouted, nothing, I searched the rooms, I went down to the basement, 'where is Teresa?' I asked, 'she died,' someone replied, 'we buried her yesterday,' 'idiots!' I shouted, 'she tricked you, don't you know what a big slut she was?' no one spoke, 'how could an angel die?' I said crying.

I opened the window and indeed there at the far end of the sky shone Teresa like a star.

Incident

     I admit that if we had to put our lives in danger, we would have done so, but that other thing, how could anyone bear it without having died first? Later the woman with the grey dress became so sorrowfully withdrawn that the heavens recognized her. 'Mary!' a voice was heard – scenes we never experienced here on earth, where do they come from?
     Standing in line, holding our little tin pots, we waited for the evening meal. And the stars began to shine one by one in the boundless sky.

Indescribable Dreams

At night I think or dream in my sleep about wonderful things, but alas in the morning I can't remember them. I realize, however, that after those indescribable dreams, whatever I write will be small and insignificant compared to them. But why can't I remember? Only a dim memory as though I had returned from another life. And on rare occasions I find again the happiness that is full of pain in some splendid psalmody – or at times in the love of neighbour.

Adolescence

There are some nights when only a single sigh separates us
    from Paradise
and other times the moon rises above the hill like a great joy
wanderings at night and the louvres through which we dimly
    saw a woman in her underwear as she was sleeping
and suddenly at the turn of the road the sadness of a lamppost
    inundated us with tears.

No one was waiting for us when we returned.

Daybreak

Father usually wore a marigold on his lapel, and mother a robe
    with pictures of ancient idylls
and when we played in the yard we would step only on the
    white slabs: this is why we never exited the dream
the Little Bear would flirt with September
oh childhood: untranslatable eternity
and God, from the tearful prayers of children who are afraid of
    the night, creates the first azure threads of the day
    which send hope to the shipwrecked.

Childhood

The house was unwell: the wall clock had an ulcer,
the unintelligible words of children at sleep as they try to
    decipher an enigma,
the farewell of a long drawn-out summer that will not return,
the eternal dreams of those who will soon be dead.
Oh Teresa, I have you within me like childhood keeps within it
    all our future stories!

Passer-by

But why is it that whenever I want to forget I hear those
 gunshots? Signs of the times, you will say,
the world in our day has become full of crime and the cypress
 trees near the railway tracks move along quietly
like those who have departed for the future. Who remembers
 them?
Our memories stretch further than what we have lived,
and I: an age-old passer-by disappearing in the depths.

Predetermination

There comes a time when you stand in the middle of the road, it is night – nothing is happening, but the distant voice of a child, the scent of jasmine from a garden, the silence of the stars interrupted by the whistling of a train make you feel as though suddenly here, at this moment, you have lived everything that was predetermined for you by God

and afterwards everything else will no longer have any meaning.

Hope

When they expelled us from Paradise, Mary wept. I then took her to the nearby hotel because we had to allow life to go on. When we came out night was falling. Mary stroke her belly. 'There is hope,' she said.

The hope that makes the world even more uncertain.

The Past

Everything ends someday. And my relatives now find
    themselves well protected where they have gone –
they have forgotten the weather, the Christmas gifts, the
    dreams,
sometimes I visit them and when I return
I rest my umbrella against the kitchen sink. My gestures sketch
    incomprehensible symbols on the wall –
oh forgotten years of cheerful companionship.

The First Day of the World

It was the first day after the ancestral sin. Mary and I had just left the old hotel where possibly she had conceived. We walked along silently. 'Mary, how will we be saved?' I asked. The sun was setting. At the city's entrance there sat a man dressed in rags with two grimy dice in his hands. 'Want to play?' he asked me.

At bottom God seemed very lonely.

Tales

   Later they come to tell you, 'the years have gone,' but I want you to count also that which has gone together with the years – who is able to bear that? And so that evening I was turning into a side street when I noticed a man being harassed by the police, he was middle-aged with a small beard, 'what's your name?' they asked him, he kept silent, 'leave him!' I said, 'I paid with my soul for him. His name is Lenin.'

  (Old tales – so that this night too might pass.)

Trojan War

The sea endless like a daydream
women beautiful like Helen
friendships uncertain, omens indecipherable
and in the morning we will wake up again
defenceless.

Stories

The night is an enlightened nation overrun by louts and poets
at the stations the new moon converses with the old trains
tell me, then, stories of horrific things, make me die from
    fright –
and sometimes we need the whole sky to cross even a single
    road.

Autumn

I dream of a statue crying in the mist, a prisoner singing
a woman not plundering her years, a child not asking
    questions.
In autumn I will gather all the leaves at my door so that my
    lost life might droop down.

A Bird at the Window

James stood at the back of the room, 'everything happened orderly,' he said and I shuddered because I knew what he meant and in autumn he sent us the last yellow leaves.

But that bird which struck the window, that beautiful bird of youth, what did it want?

Scenes from Life

From the open window the days disappear, spiders in the
 corners,
a streak of moonlight on the floor, the prudent mice rarely
 come out
a woman lights some incense – each of us has a hidden
 fortune from humiliations they've forgotten
but someday they'll remember them.

'That tree has grown old,' the gardener later said as we were
 taking down someone who had hung himself.

The Kingdom

After some fatal coincidences and many other incidents he became king of all evenings and of a few very sad afternoons. But in the mornings he had nothing to do. And this drove him one day to abandon us and go to the corner of the garden
      and hang himself.

Greetings to History

The trees are the lecterns upon which the birds rest their long-
 winded texts
the roads towards pleasure vanish at night in the infinite – as if
 we were never coming back –
but in the morning I take my hat off to everydayness which
 rewrites the Iliad from the beginning.

Morning Gaiety

Sometimes sorrow prevails in the rooms upstairs
I stay in the basement, close to fate
in the evenings the poor follow the birds in the sky
in the morning the birds follow the poor in the parks,
a beggar in the corner sings for the thousandth time
       the Odyssey of futility.

The Stranger

I was walking on the street when someone stopped in front of
> me. We didn't speak.
He only looked at me with the gaze of another era that those
> who rule our lives always have.
Then I heard his footsteps receding. And only the stars had
> remained there
on the darkened sky.

The Blind Musician

I felt like a stranger in this city even though my family had settled here from time immemorial. That's why when Helen would undress and take out her hairpins, her hair would fall down unrestrainedly and cover all the enigmas. I would struggle afterwards to find my way back. And the blind man with the flute always out on the street: he would play a soft melody which made the birds come down and peck at the small stains which the centuries leave on the marbles.

Whistling Like a Child

As we were walking along the deserted street he opened his coat and showed me his childhood face, 'for forty years now I can't part with it,' he said, 'even though I should have buried it somewhere.'

And I, the idiot, was baffled that at times he whistled in such a carefree way.

Oddities

After so many years and so many farewells I arrived at the
    final frontier
in my arms I held my little deceased cousin – I was taking her
    to pass the summer in the unknown.
My eyes were moist as though I had cried over bizarre books.

Sunset

And when God completed the creation of the world the dyer arrived to take the women's clothes for the period of mourning
and flower shops came into being one after the other. I opened the window and saw in the distance the inglorious end of the day.

III

What meaning does it have for me?
I often asked myself. I didn't know.
But I did know that as soon as I found out,
it would no longer have any meaning.

Immortality

The old comrades have not died but reside now at the far end
    of the roads –
whichever one you take you will run into them.

Ideologue

Naturally he tried to hide his crippled arm
for this reason he was always holding a flag.

Ideologue II

Each time they offered me a chair I fell into the trap.
For this reason I have been standing for years now as though
    listening to the Internationale.

Odyssey

A song sleeps on the harp until it is awoken by a strange pain and oh traveller, upon returning from the Ocean, you'll be shipwrecked amongst the roses in a garden.

Abridged Iliad

We don't truly live except at night within the dream.
And in the morning you say 'good morning,'
    they reply 'good morning.'
                        And the slaughter continues.

Oleanders

Night is falling. A street organ can be heard playing behind the trees.
Two beggars stand outside the door of twilight.
I look at the oleanders and cry...

Wedding Night

I had gone so far that I felt the sigh of God on my shoulder
the Great Bear walked quietly, leaving silver traces on the
    road.
The evenings are usually sorrowful like a journey that has
    come to an end.
Honours have no meaning whatsoever under the apple trees.

Above All, Quiet!

Like everyone, I too got to know many people – only the
      beautiful Henrietta I didn't get around to meeting
they had just forgotten her – since then I have been in a hurry,
      I want to learn, learn what? I don't know.
But at night I am scared and walk on tip-toe
      so as not to awake the old clocks.

The Dream

In the end I shut the door on them, 'what's the use of reality
    when I have the dream?' I told them,
perhaps that's why I like cemeteries, because they put an end
    to details.
A sad song at night is always a farewell.

Correspondence Interrupted

The world has become desolate, to whom might one address
    oneself?
All those with whom we could have had a brief
    correspondence have died.
                              And we first among them.

Autumn Twilight

Night was falling and at the far end of the autumnal road the
    light was diminishing more and more
as though the world were ending for good.

The Midnight Train

Sometimes the whistling of a train at night has something of
    the eternal departure –
oh don't speak – day might dawn no more.

Futile Decisions

At times I sit and think: if only I could return to the past
    to sort out some things, to finish up others.
But what difference would it make?

I am tired from so many separations, so many mornings, so
    many afternoons.

The Great Hour

There often exists something around you that is so beautiful and indefinable that you take off your coat and throw it off the bridge or you hang your hat on the lamppost as though it were the most sincere gesture of the century.

But only when they humiliate you do you hear the groaning of God.

The Ship

A woman halts on the pier. She is wearing black. She is
 intolerably beautiful. A violet sunset.
Oh I have lived with a strange feeling: that I forgot all my
 luggage in a ship
which has already sounded its horn and is setting sail...

January

A new year. What awaits us? What will it bring us?
>Dreams, ambitions, loves, enigmas.
And oh wretched calendars: after so many holidays
>you finish your days in a gutter.

April

The days drive the birds mad, the nights knock the girls over
and the deep red moon rises like the memory of a time in
>one's life that will never return.

July

The evenings usually arrive like a joy or like a river of tears
and lovers, after the splendour of an hour beneath the trees,
>return to the city, practically blind.

September

A child walks along the street, their shoulders weighed down
>by a school bag full of tiny unrealizable things.
I sit by the window and look at the rain running away with the
>loves of summer.

A Painter Who Died in Patmos

'I can't hang myself,' he grumbled, 'the great conflagration of twilight
 burns the rope.'

Disappearances

How many were not lost in the desert or in the crowd, in the sea or in some corner of the earth
while others were lost in their very own homes and no one looked for them.

People...

People who lived so secretly that when they died death found
	nothing to take.
And tonight, as always, the moon came out not suspecting
	anything.

Poets

Poor stowaways atop the wings of birds
                                        as they are falling, stricken.

The Garden

'I was sad because my heartless father had no affection nor any dreams,' my distant aunt of the garden said to me. And that would have been her entire life-story if a blossoming branch had not touched her grey hair.

The Way

After my bitter return (from where, I wonder?) I would often sit in a coffee-house, one of those of humble sorrows with long drawn-out sunsets on the windows.
And only those who died too soon never lost their way.

Simile

A poet usually resembles someone who is being mercilessly pursued on the street but manages to get into his house in time, and there, gasping for breath but with undivided attention, begins to beat the old ancestral rugs.

Wandering

And we continue the eternal wandering. As we leave no one
    bids us farewell, as we arrive no one recognizes us.
We are the ones who give meaning to the kingdom of twilight,
    but before night has fallen
they have forgotten us.

Epilogue

Unlucky as always, every time I decided to change my life there would be some delay, a postponement, a dream – the years passed. Besides I don't remember anything. And the lamp had been extinguished an eternity ago.

Poetry is for Two

'Will we come again?' I asked. The other said something but it
 didn't reach me – however, I sensed something within
 me strange and sweet. The wind blew a little. Evening.
And perhaps the whole of poetry is that answer which was not
 heard and was supplemented by the sigh of the wind
 and the gentle solitude of the moon.

Summer

A bird sat on the garden railings, it said something to the girl on the verandah, but she didn't hear. The world was buzzing with cicadas.

And then I thought that this scene will be one I will remember someday, after many years, and I will weep inconsolably.

Nuptials

There are those who walk about all alone in the oblivion and
    only as evening approaches go to the post office of the
    Great Bear.
No one knows with whom they exchange letters. But in a little
    while the moon comes out and a rose gleams like a
    betrothed girl.
Every night is a honeymoon.

Thought at Twilight

On the street we meet old men, deserters from the old wars,
on the couch a springtime hat, one of those worn by young
 women.
Each of us has a great secret and we will depart without
 finding out what it is:
  neither we, nor anyone else.

Painting

Great sunsets put so much glint in his eyes that speech has become useless.

Unknown Homeric Verses

And those who fell in love with fame are now weeping
while others who desired death are afraid
and those who were caring have nothing
yet the ones who were humiliated are the ones who know
and those who kept their distance will set out to return
    like the beautiful epochs.

Schooling

But when they finally throw us out, where will we go? And will
    anyone recognize us on the street?
At night we have need of a friendly word or a little oblivion.
The stars were our first reader.

Lethal Game

The dead are done with hopes and dreams
the silences of lovers: immense like eternities
the miracle is justice's childhood
and poetry a game where you lose it all
       that you may win an elusive star.

Thoughts

I think of the trains hurtling towards nothingness
the sea that eternally returns...

New Geography

He loved a girl who lived in Xanthi. They would not let him go. So he set up his tent on a solitary tree and wrote on it with chalk: Xanthi.

How pointless are distances!

Simple Verses

A house in which to be born
a tree by which to breathe
a verse in which to hide
and the world in which to die.

Thank You

My God, why can't I understand you? But perhaps if I understood you I would not be able to bear your burden.

My God, with this worthless reality around us you are in danger.

How am I to save you...

March

One night I was carrying a torch: we were keeping vigil for a comrade who was at death's door, his rambling speech reminding us of all the crazy dreams of an era.
At dawn we buried him hurriedly and continued our march towards Arkhangelsk or Syracuse. I don't remember which.

Tears

Roads towards great pleasures which wind up beyond time
adventures of clumsy amorous hands in the dark, the eternity
    of a touch –
our stories were eventually left half-finished like someone's
    childhood.
Someday I will shed so many tears that I will propitiate all the
    roses.

Verses

I think about the loneliness of a child playing all on their own in a park amidst the seclusion of a summer afternoon. Perhaps the most beautiful verses of a poet originated there.

Oh Sorrow...

I had to escape, otherwise I was done for, but the stranger of the railways was already waiting for me at the end of my journey. What stranger? I was the one who was defeated and I would open the doors of the halted carriages and come out from the other side of the dream.

Oh sorrow, we came to know you as children, before ever discovering the world.

The Poet's Grievance

An old sentimental candle was burning on the table
the worn-out furniture had taught me patience
only one thing, my God, I didn't experience
for I had to take care of so many leaves in spring.

Acknowledgements

'Never, never translate a poet you do not love.' This maxim by Yves Bonnefoy, a poet and accomplished translator himself, guided my decision long ago to translate the works of Tasos Leivaditis. This latest effort has been aided along the way by Konstantina Georganta's expert and thorough feedback. I also gratefully acknowledge the ongoing support of Stylianos-Petros Halas, Tasos Leivaditis' literary executor, who kindly granted permission for the publication of this translation. The original Greek text I have used is the 2015 edition published by Metronomos, in Athens, as part of the third volume of Leivaditis' collected poetry: Τάσος Λειβαδίτης, *Ποίηση, τόμος τρίτος: 1979–1990*, pp.413–560.

Notes

Street Song
In the original manuscript this was also given the title, 'Old Song'.

Sleepless Nights
This poem was also entitled in the manuscript, 'What Will Remain?'

Short Autobiography
'Resenda' was a 1930 tango composed by Lola Votti.

Passer-by
In the manuscript this poem was given a second title: 'The Future'.